365 DAYS OF POSITIVE AFFIRMATIONS

A YEAR OF POWERFUL DAILY INSPIRATIONAL THOUGHTS FOR CREATING CHANGE IN YOUR LIFE AND ATTRACTING HEALTH, WEALTH, LOVE, HAPPINESS, CONFIDENCE AND SELF-ESTEEM

NICOLE LOCKHART

D1113760

CONTENTS

SPECIAL BONUS!
Want this Bonus Book free?

Get **FREE**, unlimited access to it and all of my new books by joining the Fan Base!

SCAN WITH YOUR CAMERA TO JOIN!

I

AFFIRMATIONS AND GOAL SETTING

WHY USE AFFIRMATIONS?

Affirmations are powerful ways to change your life. It is that simple. Basically, the proven principle of "like attracts like" is just as strong as gravity. It may be harder to explain, but that doesn't make it any less powerful. Do you wake up every morning excited and ready to take on the day? If you're like me this is not always as easy as it sounds. Positive affirmations are like snow tires in the blizzard of life.

Your brain is the original computer, it's the original smartphone and much more powerful. BUT, you have to realize that what you put in, or program, is what your brain will spit out. Really, it is just a machine, complicated with feelings and emotions. Let's take charge and put in some programming that will help us get out what we actually want out of life. Health, wealth, peace, financial prosperity, enjoyable relationships, it's all possible!

Affirmations should be spoken in the present tense as if they are happening right now or coming to you plain as day "Today, I will.." or "I am..". This makes your brain think these things are already here. So now your reality has no choice but to quickly catch up.

I encourage you to write down any affirmations that really speak to you, put them in your house where you can see them multiple times throughout the day. Use colors and even stickers to awaken your mind. Your mind will respond much stronger if colors or sparkles are added. Neurologists believe that stimulating yourself visually has a greater effect on putting your goals into action, compared to non-visual stimulus. You will need to make your desires as strong as possible so that they are forced to become your reality.

This book is designed to be read daily, but it does not have to be. If you are feeling inspired, skip ahead and read some different affirmations, if you miss a day, no problem. This book can be used year over year, you can basically never get enough of these affirmations. The more you repeat them, the closer you will get to your goals, each year make a commitment to set some new goals, you can then use this book to transform your new yearly goals into reality. If you are feeling that you can't get enough affirmations, read as many as you like. The days are just a starting point to keep you on track and reading affirmations daily.

Goal Setting

Before beginning the daily affirmations, I would suggest setting out some clear goals for yourself. Then as you read each affirmation, you can apply it directly to one of your goals. I would recommend either writing down 4 or 5 master "BIG" goals and putting the list on your wall and/or creating a vision board, big or small. You can also put your list in your smartphone's notes if you are always on the go. If you are making a vision board with poster paper, get some magazines that interest you and go through them cutting out anything that you are attracted to without judging yourself. Glue the pictures to a poster paper, even one or two magazine pictures of really important things taped to your bathroom mirror are better than nothing.

Some goals might be:

- I find a new, enjoyable and lucrative career
- I meet my soulmate
- I help my body become healthy and fit
- I buy a new car
- I buy my own house
- I earn an extra $1,000 before the end of the year

Written goals should have some or all of these qualities:

- Specific
- Measurable
- Achievable
- Realistic
- Time-bound

This is known as the S.M.A.R.T. acronym for goal setting.

Now that you have determined exactly what you want, you need to state how you will do it. If your goal is to be healthy, write out a plan statement such as:

Goal: To become healthy and fit
Plan: and I will accomplish this by eating less sugar and exercising every day.

Goal: To earn $10,000 extra this year
Plan: and I will accomplish this by selling 100 wooden tables that I have made.

As much as we would like to think our goals will magically manifest themselves, with zero effort on our part, that is just not the case. This is both good news and bad news. The good news is that change will only come to people that desire it and the not-so-good news is that you actually have to make an effort to start the process. If you desire wealth, the only way to real fortune is to provide a service or sell something of value to others. This doesn't mean you have to slave away extra hard to earn extra money. Look at the most financially successful people, most of them have their businesses set up very well, so that they can sit back and enjoy themselves. You can have this as well, think about new ways to serve people. There are ways to leverage yourself so that the amount of work you do is minimal compared to the reward. You just need to be open to some new ideas.

Don't worry if you don't yet have a plan for all of your big goals. Maybe you want to buy your own house and need $100,000 for a down payment. It might take a while to come up with a viable plan. Keep this in mind as you do your daily affirmations and manifest your self a good solid plan. Plans for big goals can take time to uncover, be patient.

In addition to consciously manifesting the goals on your list or poster board, there is a huge unconscious, unexplainable power at work as well. I have a personal story, in my 20's, my cat had passed away, I wasn't even looking for a new kitten but my friend had brought me one as a gift. It was the cutest, fluffiest, little orange male kitten. I kept him and he was my cat for many years. When he was about a year old I took another look at an old poster board I had made years before receiving the kitten. As I was looking through the pictures of houses and tropical destinations. I found glued in the corner, a tiny picture I had cut out of a fluffy orange kitten. Be warned, when you start listing your goals and start taking steps to manifest them, powerful energy is involved. Like a magnet being turned on, these goals are slowly moving closer to you. Visual stimulation, adds another level of incredible power to your brain.

In addition to your big goals, I would also suggest a list of some daily attainable goals as well, for example:

- eat less sugar
- get more exercise
- practice patience
- go to bed on time

These will help you feel good on a daily basis, so that you can focus and use your energy to achieve your big goals.

So let's begin!

II

DAILY AFFIRMATIONS

1

JANUARY

January 1

"Today, I will let go of things and people that I no longer need in my life."

Maybe you need to move out some old furniture and make a new workspace or distance yourself from unsupportive people in your life. Let them go with peace and make room to embrace the new things that are coming into your life.

January 2

"I welcome and embrace change."

Change is uncomfortable, I don't think there is any way around that. Anything new will feel different, but when it's a positive change, it doesn't take long to enjoy it. Letting go of the old and letting in the new can feel strange, trust that it is the right thing to do, keep moving forward, you will begin to enjoy the change soon.

January 3

"I will create prosperity and abundance in my life by providing services or products to people that need them."

If you are wanting to increase your bank account, remember true wealth, can only come to you in return for a service or product. What can you offer other people?

January 4

"Today, I welcome all new opportunities."

When opportunity knocks, be ready. Opportunity only knocks once so get ready for when it arrives. Some people say opportunity looks a lot like work, so be ready to work hard when a golden opportunity presents itself.

January 5

"I will listen to my body today."

Do you need more sleep, more energy, or more time to yourself? Try to find a quiet space to think about what your body needs for a successful year ahead.

January 6

"Positive, supportive people are drawn to me."

Regardless of your goals, you will likely need a team. Once, you start your journey, you will meet the people that you need to help you along your path. By being positive and supportive, people with these qualities will be drawn to you.

January 7

"My ideas are valuable."

Dig deep inside yourself. What idea have you had in the past that you haven't acted on? Maybe you quickly thought "that was a bad idea, it will never work". Yet the idea has never left you, give it a chance. Use affirmations to knock out the doubt.

January 8

"I possess the ability to make smart decisions for myself."

Even if you feel like some of your decisions have not worked out for the best, it's never too late to make some decisions from your heart. Listen quietly to what your heart is wanting for your future.

January 9

"I trust the journey that is bringing me to my goals."

Once you have set some goals, your path to them is also set, and it doesn't always make sense. Sometimes we have to get rid of old baggage or things that are no longer useful in our lives before we can start the productive part of our journey. Know that your journey is right on course.

January 10

I have a solid plan to reach my goals, and I'm sticking to it!

Persistence will get you there! Remember, if you are still waiting to uncover your plan, by repeating this, it will come to light soon, be patient. Try to think outside of the box, do some brainstorming to help find a clear, viable plan.

January 11

"My self-confidence is increasing, I am proud of myself."

Me, myself and I. It was you at the start of your life and it will be you and yourself at the end. Once you have committed to making changes in your life, you will begin to trust yourself. You will be the pillar of strength that you have always needed.

January 12

"I design my life and I am taking charge."

Nobody else is going to do it for you. Maybe it's time to step it up, more goals, more affirmations and more trust in your journey that is bringing you closer to your goals.

January 13

"I have all that I need to make today a productive and successful day."

What resources do you have at your disposal? If you aren't clear on specific work for today, do some behind-the-scenes work. Market research for a new project or reading about health. If you choose to have a day of rest, consider this to also be a success.

January 14

"Money comes quickly and easily into my life."

This is one of my favorites, if you desire more financial gain, write this affirmation everywhere to remind yourself to repeat it.

January 15

"I am persistent in whatever I do."

Slow and steady wins the race. Pace yourself, you don't need to do everything all at once. Persistence pays, think of the children's story "The Tortoise and the Hare", persist and persevere and rest as well.

January 16

"I believe in myself."

If you don't who will? Repeat this if doubt is creeping in, and remind yourself that you have your back and you will support yourself through everything that comes up.

January 17

"My confidence is increasing, I have much to offer the world."

You, yes you, are an important part of this world. Every unique individual has something amazing to offer. Think about drawing a picture or writing a poem. This is just a physical example of something you can make that could be around for hundreds of years.

January 18

"I can do anything I put my mind to."

Whatever goals you have chosen, if they exist on this earth, you can accomplish them. Be patient, bigger goals might take longer and require more extreme plans and preparation.

January 19

"Today, I am thankful for everything in my life."

Take a look around, you likely have a roof over your head and food in the fridge. You have a lot to be thankful for, thankfulness and gratitude open the gates to fulfilling your goals.

January 20

"I rely on myself."

You might be a young adult wanting to be more independent or perhaps you feel trapped in your job or current relationship. You have the power to get yourself out of any situation and become self-reliant.

January 21

"I choose to be kind to everyone that I encounter."

A little kindness goes a long way. Do your best to exude kindness to everyone you meet, kindness is a quality that comes back to you exponentially. It doesn't cost anything and is very powerful.

January 22

"I am discovering interesting and exciting new paths each and every day."

The world is full of endless possibilities, when we get caught up on the hamster wheel of daily life, it is hard to see them. Today, take a different route to work or to check your mail. Look around at all the opportunities that are close by.

January 23

"I am wise."

See the world for what it is. No need to protect people or sugar-coat things. With each experience you have, your judgment will improve. Take some time to think about the situation before you reach a conclusion or speak about it.

January 24

"I am proud of myself."

Others may not agree with your choices, so you need to be your own champion. Be proud of the progress you have made so far. As you uncover your strengths and continue to put them into practice, your confidence will increase.

January 25

"I am courageous and will never back down from what I believe in."

Always do what you know to be right. Don't be bullied or pushed around by people with their own agenda. This includes your plans to your goals, believe in them and don't ever stop.

January 26

"I desire wealth."

In order for wealth to come to you, you need to make your desire extremely strong. Think of how it would feel to have all the wealth you dream of. Add to your vision board or make a cut-out with the number of dollars you wish to acquire. Make it colorful and sparkly, this will put your brain in overdrive attraction mode.

January 27

"I am getting on with my life."

Sometimes we feel held back by certain people or circumstances in our lives. Repeating this will help those blockages fade away. Put on those snow tires and get going with your own life!

January 28

"I am worthy of a healthy body."

Having a healthy body is important for enjoying the goals you have worked so hard for. Make a decision to be more aware of what you are putting into your body.

January 29

"I am patient."

Good things come to those who wait. This doesn't mean just sit around and do nothing. Good things come to those who are persistent and patient. Let's be real, a new job or car could take months to procure, a new house could take a year or more to achieve or your soulmate could show up at any time. They will come when you are ready to receive them. Trust that it is all working perfectly.

January 30

"I choose to be peaceful."

You can be strong and brave and still choose peace, you don't need to fight with others to be successful. Just carry on your path and most problems will resolve themselves.

January 31

"I am planting the seeds in my mind today for my ultimate future."

We reap what we sow. Now is the time to sow seeds for the future. Change doesn't happen overnight, but planting seeds now, and nurturing them, will give you the results you have been dreaming of.

2

FEBRUARY

February 1

"I am creating the life I want and I am enjoying it now."

Take some time today to do something out of the ordinary for yourself. Get your favorite expensive coffee drink, or buy a piece of clothing that brings a smile to your face.

February 2

"I am open to new ways of improving my health."

Maybe it's time to order some new vitamins or try the new juice bar down the street. Maybe you've been thinking about changing your diet or incorporating more exercise into your day. Get creative, find some new and fun ways to improve your health.

February 3

"I am creating all the success and prosperity I desire."

Gather some magazines or newspapers, cut out pictures that speak to you, a new car, a new house, a pet, a picture of a relationship you would like to pursue or even a picture of a coffee cup that you are visually attracted to. Glue them to a poster board or tape them to your wall if you don't have glue. Surround yourself with pictures of your future. If you have already made a vision board, you can add to it anytime.

February 4

"I am brave and I am creating positive change in my life."

Baby steps, the beginning of anything is always the hardest. When doubt and despair creep in, be armed with some good affirmations that speak to you, so you can reprogram your brain.

February 5

"I am proud of my actions."

Others may not agree with your choices and actions, especially if they can't see where all your new plans are headed. What you think of yourself is all that matters. Choose your actions carefully, and be incredibly proud of yourself.

February 6

"I will celebrate this day with gratitude and joy."

Whatever this day brings, be grateful. Gratitude opens the floodgates to unlimited potential in all areas of your life. Being gracious will help you exude joy, try to spread some joy to others.

February 7

"Today I stay in my lane, and don't compare myself to others."

Think of horses running a race, they all have blinders on so that they stay in their lane and don't look at what their neighbors are doing, blinders are the only way a horserace will work. Try to put some blinders on, and think only of your own goals. Everybody has their own set of challenges and you don't need to concern yourself with their progress.

February 8

"I am finding ways to afford the things I need and want."

Instead of compromising your needs and wants, find ways to accomplish them. Be open to new opportunities to create wealth. Making a vision board will help find a means to your goals.

February 9

"I am feeling happy and successful and feel grateful for my life."

Even if you're not feeling happy and successful today, this affirmation will attract happiness and success, "like attracts like". By saying this you are resonating with happiness and success and bringing more of them into your life.

February 10

"I love my body shape, it is perfect and the way it is intended to be."

Although we can not change our body's shape or height, we can change what we put into it. Try to eat some more fresh fruits and vegetables, your body will thank you!

February 11

"I have faith in my abilities to achieve my goals."

Once you learn what your passions are, you will be aligned with your purpose. You will see that your abilities actually match, and are designed to reach your goals.

February 12

"I am learning new things that will result in bringing me happiness, freedom, and purpose."

You will have to learn some new things. The first of which is reprogramming your brain with affirmations. Then you may have to learn new skills for your new job or some new daily routines that will contribute to your physical health.

February 13

"I trust myself, I am confident that I am doing the right thing."

Which comes first, trust or confidence? They go hand in hand, the more you trust yourself, the more confident you can be, and the more confident you are, the more your self-trust will grow. As you continue to manifest change, both will increase.

February 14

"I attract real love into my life."

Real love is doing things for others, because you know it is important to them or it is something they enjoy, and expecting nothing in return. Pay it forward at the drive-through or do something for a family member that is needed and appreciated. This will be reciprocated in ways we can't imagine.

February 15

"I am free."

If you are wanting change in your life, chances are you are feeling trapped in one or more areas of your life. While you are enduring your present situation, know that you really are free, you are just disposing of residual garbage, which can take time. Go for a walk outside, feel the sun and the wind on your face. You are free.

February 16

"I am consistently becoming more successful."

Success can occur in any area of your life. By focussing on affirmations daily, writing some of your favorites in a visible place, and making a vision board for the areas of your life that you want to change, these things are forced to come closer to you.

February 17

"I release all negativity."

It is easy to get in the habit of cursing at slow drivers or being easily annoyed for whatever reason. Let these negative feelings pass through you, there is no need to react or hold on to them.

February 18

"I have a lot to offer the world and receive fulfillment in return."

There are times when we feel insignificant, like the world would continue regardless of what we do. This is doubt and despair creeping in, pick your favorite affirmations to fight and get ready to provide a service or product to people that need them, you will be rewarded in return.

February 19

"This morning, I wake up ready for a new day of exciting possibilities."

Be open to new things, if someone strikes up a conversation while you are waiting in a lineup, listen to what they have to say. You might just stumble upon some unexpected inspiration.

February 20

"Today, I will endure."

Some things just need to run their course. Maybe you are wanting to create a new career or find a new place to live. While you are manifesting this into your life, you still have to attend your old job. Endurance is an incredible quality to possess. Know that enduring your present situation is bringing you closer to your goals.

February 21

"I am worthy of joy in my life."

Maybe it's been a while since you have delighted with glee. As an adult, these opportunities are few and far between, observe some kids playing, or go to a park and watch the wildlife playing around. You will be reminded that joy is one of the simplest emotions.

February 22

"I always attract only the best positive people into my life."

If you repeat this today, and any other day, you will find you have nothing in common with negative people. Unsupportive people that are judging you or enjoy watching other people fail will fade away and disappear out of your life.

February 23

"I will make impressive contributions to the world today."

Whether it's going to work and doing your job, drawing a picture, or making an invention. Know that whatever it is, it is valuable to the world. Without your efforts the world would just be rocks and trees, know that whatever you have done today is important.

February 24

"I am always creating and looking for new opportunities."

If you don't see a new opportunity in front of you right now, then make one! With your goals in mind, go to a bookstore or look online for a new topic that interests you.

February 25

"I am not afraid of making mistakes."

Actually there are no such things as mistakes. Maybe you regret a certain choice you made. This regret will make sure it never happens again. Look at the "mistake" as a learning opportunity, one you have now learned and never have to experience again.

February 26

"I am calm and content."

Remember to breathe deeply, oxygen is life, it will calm us and heal us. If you are feeling exasperated, take some time to practice deep breathing.

February 27

"I choose to only let positive thoughts into my mind."

Your brain is the original computer, input results in output. Choose thoughts that will get you where you want to be. If I feel doubt or despair creeping in, I go straight to repeating affirmations. It is a good idea to have a few favorites written on the wall or saved in your smartphone for doubting emergencies.

February 28

"My needs and wants are important to me."

They may not be important to others, so don't fool yourself into thinking others really care about what makes your heart happy. They are often too busy thinking about their own path. Only you are responsible for fulfilling your wants and needs.

February 29

"Practicing gratitude brings me joy."

Reflect on the things that you are thankful for. Buy some thank you cards to have on hand to give to people to show your gratitude.

3

MARCH

March 1

"I love the way I look."

Accepting and loving the way you look is essential for happiness. The things that you were born with and can not change, make you - you. But there are some things you can change, how about a new haircut or color, or some new clothes?

March 2

"I am focused on my work and welcome new work opportunities."

Think about some other ways you can provide the service or product that you specialize in. There may be other income streams just waiting for you to tap into them.

March 3

"I have everything I need to face any challenges that arise."

Challenges always have a way of popping up, when we view them as an opportunity for learning, we have the ability to make them disappear forever. It is the challenge that is overlooked that continues to show up.

March 4

"I am living my life with purpose."

Doing meaningful work will harmonize with the forces that will bring you what you are wanting to achieve. Whether it is your full-time job that is meaningful to your soul or your hobby, do more of it.

March 5

"My relationships are healthy."

By making this affirmation a part of your inner programming, unhealthy relationships will fade away. There will no longer be an unhealthy connection to keep them going.

March 6

"Today, I will have success."

Keep an eye open for even small successes, maybe you remembered to put less sugar in your coffee or made a healthy choice for a snack. However small, these are important successes.

March 7

"Today, I focus on positive progress."

Take a minute to pat yourself on the back, you have already come so far. The beginning is the hardest and you will soon see the fruits of your labor.

March 8

"I am creating my destiny."

You are the captain of your own ship. Set your goals and get ready to achieve them! Don't settle for anything less and do your best to block out negative people.

March 9

"Today, I let go of fear forever."

As you become more self-reliant, fear will disappear, know that you will always be there for yourself, and you can get through anything that comes your way.

March 10

"I abandon old habits that no longer serve me."

Do you need to stop some bad habits? Replacing them with something positive is the best way to leave them far behind. For example, if you have a donut every day for breakfast, find a fruit or a sugar-free treat that you can eat instead of the donut.

March 11

"I breathe good energy in and breathe bad energy out."

This might take a while to get right because you are focussing on breathing and thinking at the same time. Find a quiet space and give it a try.

March 12

"I'm in charge of creating my path in life."

Parents are the worst for pushing their hopes and dreams onto their children. We are each born with unique skills and gifts, you are still probably figuring out your own. So don't let anyone else tell you what you should or should not be doing.

March 13

"I will be patient with myself while I heal."

Maybe there is a part of your past that still presents itself today, a limiting belief or a childhood tragedy. Look for ways to heal, take your time, and treat yourself with love and patience.

March 14

"I earn money doing what I love."

Even if you have a job that you don't especially like, start up a side gig that you love. It doesn't matter how big or small. Once you start, you will be helped along your way.

March 15

"I attract success and happiness."

That's right, your new energy is attracting success and happiness right now, can you feel it? Do something for yourself today, a walk at your favorite park or dig out some old songs that remind you of how far you have come.

March 16

"I am creating a healthy body by talking about and thinking about my wellness."

The six best doctors in the world are sunlight, rest, exercise, diet, self-confidence and friends."

~Steve Jobs

March 17

"I feel happy even though I am alone."

Maybe you are still searching for your soulmate or even just a kindred spirit. Remember, a cup of tea and a good book are a close second. Take care of yourself, order your favorite dinner, put on your favorite movie and have an enjoyable evening for one.

March 18

"I receive unexpected opportunities."

Networking with supportive people and taking risks will help you create meaningful opportunities in your life. Sometimes opportunities look like a lot of work, don't pass them up because of this. If an opportunity is in front of you, grab it!

March 19

"I let go of what I can not change."

Have you been holding on to the hope that someone or something will change? Chances are, if it hasn't happened yet, it may never will, time to let go and move on with your own goals.

March 20

"I am ready to begin my journey to my goals."

Not going all the way and not starting are two mistakes people make in their lives. One step in front of the other. Slowly but surely you will get there.

March 21

"I am grateful to be alive."

We are all so lucky to be living right now, it's the best time in the history of mankind. Be grateful that you are alive now and take care of your body so it will last a long time.

March 22

"I have valuable talents and skills."

Do you have untapped skills or talents that have never realized their full potential? Maybe you really enjoyed woodworking in high school, or baking. These are just some great examples of modern-day side gigs, and many times they can become a full-time job.

March 23

"I teach others to believe in me because I believe in myself."

If you have doubters in your life, remember living well is the best revenge. We don't need to be vengeful at all, but stop worrying about what others think, their thoughts about you will only change when they actually see change within yourself. Focus on yourself.

March 24

"I am feeling confident and strong today."

This affirmation is a protective one, hopefully by now you are feeling more strong and confident in general. By repeating this, you are shutting out doubt and despair, which are just waiting for a chance to creep into your mind.

March 25

"My past is not an indication of my future."

You have chosen to make changes in your life, don't get stuck remembering things that have held you back in the past, the past is over, while you may have to come to terms with events that occurred, do not let these events limit your future. I tell myself "next time, I will do it differently" if a past choice continues to bother me.

March 26

"I am at peace with myself."

Do you suffer from an inner struggle? Something that you know isn't good for you but you just can't stop doing it? Take a step back and try to view yourself from a distance. What could you tell yourself to encourage positive change? There are also apps for changing habits that many people find helpful.

March 27

"The decisions I make help bring me closer to my goals."

Trust that you are making the right decisions, sometimes it might look like you are completely detouring the right path to your goals. Making decisions from your heart will always move you in the right direction.

March 28

"Today, I will forgive."

Although I am a firm believer in only forgiving those who have asked for forgiveness. If they haven't accepted that they did something wrong and hurt you why give them your forgiveness? But there is something else you can do, you can thank them FOR GIVING you that experience. There are some people that you simply can not trust, but thanking them for the experience melts away any resentment you are carrying.

March 29

"I can do it all."

Do you ever have moments where you feel overwhelmed? For me, I usually wake up early morning worrying and thinking about all the things on my to-do list. Repeat this affirmation, there is no need to worry, you can do it all. One thing at a time.

March 30

"I am in charge of my life."

If you are part of a family or work-group that sees you as a part of the whole, it can be difficult to do what is best for you. Perhaps you can find a way to forge your path while still being a part of the group, but if not, consider being brave and venturing off on your own.

March 31

"I am excited for the future."

Feel excited, act excited, talk excitedly, enthusiasm and excitement are contagious. An excited state of mind will be one of your super-powers to help you reach your goals.

4

APRIL

April 1

"Every day is becoming easier, I am getting closer to my goals."

Have faith, it will all come together. One step at a time. Think of climbing a long winding staircase, you can't see the top, but each step brings you closer. Know that you are on your way and try to enjoy the journey.

April 2

"Difficulties make me stronger."

Do you ever have days where things just seem to go wrong? You forgot your password, your bank card is not working or you dropped and spilled something by accident? Stay calm, these things will only make you stronger. Maybe you need to put in place some backups to ensure these things don't happen again.

April 3

"I deeply love and accept myself."

This affirmation is used in EFT (Emotional Freedom Technique), which is a whole other topic all together. Self-love and self-acceptance are key to healing and moving on. You need to know that you have your own back. Know that you are there for yourself and you can conquer almost any challenge.

April 4

"Today, I give extra care and love to the parts of me that need it."

Whether you are suffering from aches and pains or something more serious. Focus on the part of you that needs extra care. Be open to new ways of creating health and eliminating sickness in your body.

April 5

"I make smart decisions."

Have faith in yourself. The decisions you make are based on your experiences and what you think is best. Even if your choice doesn't turn out how you had hoped, you will still learn something, making you smarter. Next time do it differently.

April 6

"I'm in charge of how I react to others."

When we are cultivating peace and positivity in our lives, we can sometimes run into people that find it necessary to be difficult. Acknowledge that you are no longer playing that game, excuse yourself to go do something important or tell them you will have to call them back later.

April 7

"Each day is becoming easier."

You have been committed to change now for a while. Although there may be some rough days in the beginning while your present situation is aligning with your future goals, once this passes, every day will be easier.

April 8

"I am creating change."

That is what this is all about, creating change and you are doing it now, affirmations and goals will set you in motion for change.

April 9

"I follow my bliss."

It's true that sometimes we have to do things we don't especially like doing. Going to the dentist or paying taxes. These things will seem much more insignificant if you can identify your true bliss and passions. Look around, what colors do you like to see? Do you enjoy plants in your home? Or maybe go shopping for a new framed feature picture for your living room. Whatever inspires you, do more of that.

April 10

"I appreciate everything I have in my life."

Gratitude is the essence of fulfillment. Appreciating and being grateful for everything in your life, even if it's something you need to let go of, will pave the way to fulfilling your dreams and goals.

April 11

"I desire health."

Do you take steps every day to ensure your body remains healthy? Without health, it is difficult to accomplish anything. Make a commitment to yourself to spend a certain amount of time devoted to your health. Whether you want more energy or you feel fine, don't let this slip, it is one of the most important things.

April 12

"Today, I will watch for a sign, something calling me to investigate further."

It could be an old song on the radio or an add on a billboard, look for something that resonates with you, this will help guide you for the year ahead.

April 13

"Today, great things are coming to me."

Try to focus on the wonderful small things that come into your life today. A cup of coffee or a phone call from a friend.

Being gracious for the small things will open the door to bigger things.

April 14

"I rely on myself."

Have you ever felt like your hands are tied because you have to rely on someone else? Like you can't make the choice you want to because you need to make someone else happy? If one of your goals is independence and self-reliance, quietly hatch your plan, before you know it you will be able to assert your own needs and wants.

April 15

"I welcome new opportunities into my life."

Try to be open to new business ventures and new ways to make friends or meet people. You can still be smart and safe while exploring new opportunities.

April 16

"I believe the universe is giving me exactly what I need, when I need it."

Once you have made your plan for reaching your goals, and have made it clear how you will work towards getting there, the universe will conspire to make sure you succeed. We can't always see how or why things are happening, but trust it is unfolding perfectly.

April 17

"The small steps I make will get me to my goals."

If it seems to be slow going, be persistent, you will achieve your goals. Focus, patience and persistence will get you there. It is the small pieces that will make the big picture.

April 18

"I am feeling energetic today."

Start the day with some stretches and deep breathes of fresh air. Try to drink more water and only drink coffee in the morning. Make choices to eat food that gives you pure energy instead of slowing you down.

April 19

"I am strong and brave, I have the courage to face my fears."

You can do it! Many of us have a voice telling us that we can't achieve a certain success, repeating these words will help drown out that voice and build your courage.

April 20

"I will not let anyone or anything stop me from pursuing my goals."

Don't be distracted by nearby pitfalls, focus your energy on your own path. If challenges arise along your journey, deal with them. Be aware of the difference between your challenges and the challenges others face.

April 21

"Today, I promise to listen to my needs."

Try to listen quietly to uncover what your heart and soul are yearning for. It is hard to listen with the daily hustle and bustle, but try to take a few minutes to sit outdoors in a park or a forest. Find somewhere quiet without distractions, close your eyes and listen quietly to the thoughts that enter your mind. Bring a pen and a paper to note these golden ideas.

April 22

"I am choosing to make changes in my life and reach my goals."

If you always do what you've always done, you will stay right where you are. Congratulations on deciding to make changes and get the life you've always wanted.

April 23

"Today, I am looking for new ideas that inspire me."

Take some time to shop online or go to a store and just look around. Don't judge, just see what your eyes are drawn to.

April 24

"Today, I release any negative beliefs I have about attracting money."

Thoughts like "money is scarce" or "you need to hold on to money" are just not true. There is enough money for everyone. Money is just a physical representation of how you contribute to society, what product or service can you offer? And who can you help with extra money that has already come to you?

April 25

"I am courageous and I believe in myself."

You have the ability to do whatever you set your mind to. Stand tall and face your fears, nobody else will do it for you. Push through, your goals are waiting for you.

April 26

"Change comes at the right time."

We don't know how change will unfold in our lives. Often we have to set into motion our plans for reaching our goals and then eliminate things that are holding us back. Once we actually see some results it is very exciting! Be patient if it hasn't happened yet.

April 27

"I embrace every season of my life."

You may feel like you want to fast forward through certain parts of your life. Try to enjoy every part, each one is setting the stage for future, more gainful seasons. Could Spring arrive without Winter?

April 28

"I am persistent in making my dreams a reality."

Persistence is continuous positive action in spite of difficulties. Keep your eye on the prize.

April 29

"I will not make excuses for anything."

Too cold to walk to work, too tired? Healthy food is too expensive? Throw out those excuses and just do it. Excuses will keep you stuck forever.

April 30

"I love and appreciate my body."

You only get one body. Learn to love and appreciate it regardless of its shortfalls, problems or limitations. Make the best of the body you were given and take care of it.

5

MAY

May 1

"I am open to new ideas that will contribute to my success."

Once you've set some goals for yourself, either written goals or on a vision board, the next step is working on your plan to achieving them. You never know where new ideas might come from, so be open to new ideas that you previously had never considered.

May 2

"I appreciate my efforts."

In the beginning especially, it can seem like all work and no results. Thank yourself for all that you do. Buy yourself something, or do something for yourself that you enjoy, to thank yourself for all your hard work so far.

May 3

"I love to exercise."

Even if you don't, repeating this will help change your mindset. Look into some new forms of exercise that you enjoy. Yoga, a hike or swimming perhaps.

May 4

"I am working towards financial freedom."

Work on your budget, pay off your credit cards and try to save a little bit each month. Work on your BIG goals and remember to give some money to those in need when extra money starts coming in.

May 5

"My curses are actually my blessings."

Is there something you have viewed negatively about your life? Maybe you were born with a disability or a learning challenge. Since you are an expert in living with this challenge why not try to help others? You could write a book or support people that need it.

May 6

"I attract positive people into my life."

Be the positive person that you want to attract. Focus on the good in your life and comment on other's successes. Be gracious and talk to yourself in a positive way.

May 7

"I know I will reach my goals."

Maybe you still have in the back of your mind "maybe I will and maybe I won't". Put an end to that now. Make a commitment that you WILL reach your goals.

May 8

"I am creating positive changes in my life."

In addition to your master goal list, I would suggest creating a daily one as well. Daily goals could be more exercise or eating less sugar. Replacing unhealthy things with something better, is the best way to change your habits.

May 9

"I approve of my choices."

It's your life. No one has to live with your choices except you. You will find there are many people who will want to put in their two cents about what choice you should make. Thank them for their concern and then do what you choose.

May 10

"My sleep is relaxing and refreshing."

Some tips for sleeping better are: staying up a bit later so that when you fall asleep it will be a deeper sleep, avoid napping, only drink coffee in the morning and look into supplements like melatonin if you still have trouble sleeping.

May 11

"Each day, I put my plan into action to consistently work towards my goals."

Rome wasn't built in a day, be patient with yourself. As long as you are doing consistent actions every day, you will reach your goals.

May 12

"I believe my body wants to heal itself."

Your body is amazing, including having the ability to heal itself. Give it the right nutrients and conditions and it will give you all it has.

May 13

"I am fearless."

Facing your fears is more easily said than done. But when we avoid our fears, they actually grow and dominate us. The only way "out" is "through". Make some manageable steps to break through your fear and don't be afraid to get professional help from a therapist if fear is still holding you back.

May 14

"I focus on my desires and goals."

Make your goals and dreams the focus of your day so that their attraction towards you is magnetically strong. Once they become a part of your mindset, they will come to you with magnetic force.

May 15

"I am open to a shift in energy in my life."

Quite often when we are creating change in our lives, we need to undergo an energy shift. It will feel like everything and nothing changing at the same time. Basically, you will be getting a new outlook or perspective that will allow you to accomplish the goals you have set. When it happens, you will be in super-power mode.

May 16

"I am aligned with my purpose."

Some people search their whole lives and never find their true purpose. Don't be one of them. Listen quietly to your inner voice and remember the times in your life when you were most fulfilled. Volunteering your time will also help you find out what truly matters to you.

May 17

"I am courageous and brave."

Just go for it! Easier said than done. Bravery is a skill, the more you face your fears, the braver you will become. Try something out of your comfort zone, go for a jog in the park, or sign up for a course and learn something new.

May 18

"I am proud of myself for sticking to my plan."

It takes a lot of determination and dedication to see your plan through to fruition. Written goals, a positive attitude and rewarding yourself will help. Congratulate yourself for your hard work!

May 19

"I am patient while change is evolving in my life."

As we work towards our goals, we can't always understand the way our circumstances are unfolding. Trust that it is working out perfectly for you, and every event that happens is happening to get you closer to your goals.

May 20

"My hard work is rewarded with money."

The only surefire way to sustainable wealth is providing a valuable service or product to others. Once you are doing work that you are passionate about, people will be lining up to give you their money.

May 21

"I am feeling vibrant and full of energy today."

Vibrance implies energy is flowing in and out of you. If you have not been feeling vibrant lately, try meditating, spending time in nature, getting more sleep and try to smile more.

May 22

"Day by day, I am achieving my goals."

The journey of a thousand miles starts with a single step is an ancient Chinese proverb, and still rings true today. All that is needed is consistent effort and you will arrive at your destination.

May 23

"I am imagining how I will feel when I achieve my goals."

Find a quiet place to envision how you will feel when you have enough money to do what you please. Enough money to take that trip, buy that car or give some to someone in need. Perhaps your goals are to feel free, imagine how you will feel on a road trip with no obligations to worry about.

May 24

"An abundant life is normal for me."

By telling yourself that abundance is normal, your mind will believe you and abundance will easily flow to you. Reconsider what you think abundance is, when we align with our purpose, abundance naturally flows.

May 25

"I am courageous."

The true test of a person's character is their reaction under fire. How will you react when challenges try to derail you. Will you stand strong and soldier on or run and hide?

May 26

"Today, I will look for a new project that I enjoy."

Is there a hobby that you've enjoyed in the past and has been shelved for a busy lifestyle? Or something new that you've always wanted to try? Take some time out of your day to work on something for no reason other than enjoyment.

May 27

"I am ready to benefit from all the hard times I have overcome in my life."

For every sorrow, there is a joy. These emotions have an incredible way of balancing. Think of the hard things you have overcome, some of us have a longer list than others. It's time to benefit from the things we have learned and use them to our advantage or to help others in similar situations.

May 28

"I am my biggest fan."

Try not to criticize yourself or be hard on yourself, supporting yourself is crucial to your success. Be proud of your accomplishments and congratulate yourself when you have a small success.

May 29

"Money comes to me with ease."

Work on becoming a money magnet. Some suggestions are: counting your money, putting up pictures of money around your house and always giving money to those in need when you have extra.

May 30

"I possess everything I need to be successful."

Everything you need, you already have. Maybe you haven't awoken some parts of yourself that are ready to spring into action. Be patient and supportive with yourself, and be open to ideas that pop up in your mind. You never know where they will lead.

May 31

"I take time to nourish my body and give it everything it needs."

If you are always on the go and have a hard time accessing good food, buy a bag of apples or oranges and keep them in your car. Nature has created most fruits with their own wrappers so you can easily bring some along with you.

6

JUNE

June 1

"I work on my plans every day until I reach my goals."

Your plan is your path to your goal. It's the yellow brick road, the path to a miracle. Stick to it and make some progress every day.

June 2

"My desires are on fire and burning hot."

In order to reach your goals, you must make your desires burning hot. Put your vision board near your bed so you can see it before you go to sleep and first thing when you wake up. If you can't sleep, stare at it. Imagine how you will feel when you have everything you want.

June 3

"Today, I will do the next right thing."

It is easy to get overwhelmed by all that goes on in a day as well as manifesting your goals. Think of a car on a long journey at night, it is dark and you can only see a short distance ahead of you. You know you have a destination, but you need to focus on the steps in front of you right now or you will never arrive. What needs to be done today? Get it done and cross it off your to-do list.

June 4

"I am transforming my life."

Many things are changing in your life. Don't be surprised if some things in your life appear to malfunction or stop working. When your energy changes, it affects everything around you. Some things just don't stack up anymore, time to upgrade them with things that are useful to you now.

June 5

"I attract everything I need for my journey to my goals."

You will need plenty of help along the way. Be open to accepting it from helpful people, or spend some time shop-

June 12

"I am patiently waiting for all my planets to align."

You are making changes in several areas of your life and so it takes time for it all to come together and create a new harmonic life for yourself. One day everything will come together and you will be pleasantly shocked.

June 13

"I am manifesting my goals into my life."

You may have days where not much seems to happen towards reaching your goals. Continue to manifest them with your affirmations, vision boards and lists. We can't always see the progress but it is happening.

June 14

"Today, I pursue my desires."

Take some time today to really think about and feel your goals. How would you feel driving that new car? How would you feel lying on a beach and not being concerned with the worries of day-to-day life? Feel the sun and wind on your face. Never give up on your desires.

June 15

"I am creating my future."

You are the creator of your reality, although you can only do so much to change your circumstances today, you can plant seeds that you will reap in the future. Get planting!

June 16

"I am attracting success."

Being successful means creating results. Results don't always come instantly, be patient, you are attracting the outcome that you desire.

June 17

"I am being my authentic self, I make choices based on what I want."

You might have people in your life that always want to throw in their two cents about what you should be doing. This can get confusing and distracting from what you really want. This is why lists and vision boards are so important, to make you focus on what you know YOU want.

June 18

"I intentionally follow my plan to reach my goals every day."

Remember the plan is the actions you are have laid out and must take to reach your goals. Action is a powerful force bringing your goals closer to you.

June 19

"I respect this season of my life."

The longest day of the year is approaching and summer is here. Which season of your life are you in? Rest, growth, reflection, sowing or reaping?

June 20

"My life is purposeful and important."

If you live in a big city or even a small one, it is easy to feel insignificant at times. Know that you are just as important as anyone else and it is your birthright as a human being to fulfill YOUR dreams.

June 21

"I give and receive love."

Giving and receiving are essential parts of the flow of energy. Although they are separate actions, they need to work together to create your abundant life. You may need to practice each independently to keep love circulating. If either giving or receiving is blocked, it will block your whole flow of love.

June 22

"I am patient with my body while it heals itself."

Most things either get better or get worse. Nothing really stays the same. Make steps to improve your health every day for the better. Give your body proper nourishment and exercise and, in most cases, it will do the rest.

June 23

"I believe in myself."

Being supportive of yourself is a huge part of reaching your goals. You need to know that you are your biggest supporter. Don't ever let yourself down. Unwaveringly believe in yourself!

June 24

"I am financially independent."

There is hardly a better feeling than having your own money to do what you choose with. Financial independence remains a dream for many. Get to work on your plan for creating extra wealth, and when money comes in, invest some, give some away and enjoy some as well.

June 25

"I motivate myself to follow my plan to reach my goals."

Usually, we try to focus on positive things and our new future. If you are feeling this isn't really enough to motivate yourself, try the opposite. Think about living in poverty and poor health and all the pain and problems that will arise if you don't get to work and reach your goals. The time for action is now!

June 26

"I am passionate about my work."

What would you do if you had a million dollars? This question has been used by many to find out what they would do if they didn't need to think about rent or the mortgage. So what would you be doing? Your answer holds the key to achieving your goals. Try to identify your true passion projects that inspire you, then think about how you could share them with others.

June 27

"I am in control of my life."

When circumstances feel out of control, either globally or locally, you might really need to repeat this all day. Some other ideas to help you feel more in control are: help other people, make some art or a physical project and also to appreciate the events occurring and learn from them.

June 28

"Achieving my goals is easy, because I stick to my plan."

Once you have your plan firmly in place. Do not waver from it, you can make adjustments along the way, but do not quit. Your plan is the path to your dreams.

June 29

"My body feels stronger each and every day."

Your health is key to enjoying your success that you are working so hard for. Remember to take time daily to tend to the needs of your body. Even if you feel fine, exercise and nutrition should be priorities in your life.

June 30

"I am brave and I stand up for myself."

If you come across someone trying to push you down or put you back in your place, this affirmation is especially important for you. You don't even need to utter a word, what is the use in talking to someone like this? Your brave actions will determine your future freedom.

7

JULY

July 1

"I am achieving greatness."

However you measure greatness you can make it your reality. Maybe you want 7 figures in your bank account or finding your soulmate is your goal. Every human being is capable of greatness, if you are committed to sticking to your plan.

July 2

"Money comes to me easily and effortlessly."

Let wealth know that it is welcome to reside with you. With this affirmation, you will become a magnet for wealth.

July 3

"Everything is possible."

If you can dream it, you can achieve it. In fact, the more you dream or think of your goal, the closer it will come to you. Once you have established some key goals and plans for reaching them, you can work on finding practical ways to achieve them.

July 4

"I make great choices."

In most countries, free choice is a human right. Don't ever let anyone try to shame you for a choice you have made. Even if your choice resulted in dismal failure. Learning from failure is a hugely important part of achieving success. Failure is very valuable.

July 5

"I am good at multitasking, I get a lot done."

Usually, our goals and dreams involve some kind of leisure time. Lying by a pool or on a beach. In order to have time to rest we need to make the most of our work time. Try to accomplish many things at once, don't overwhelm yourself, but try to think about outsourcing or delegating out some tasks that others can easily and quickly do for you.

July 6

"I believe I have value to offer the world."

There is only one you. You were created with a set of unique skills and talents that only you possess. Think about times in your life where you have felt important, maybe volunteering somewhere or helping a neighbor. What makes you feel valued? Do more of that.

July 7

"I am grateful for my body."

The body is the temple of the soul. Whether it is big or small, tall or short, treat it with the utmost gratitude, it is your body that allows your mind to achieve your goals.

July 8

"I am compassionate with myself and others."

Be kind, understanding and patient with yourself and others. Nobody gets it right every time, in fact most successes are the result of many failures. This is how we learn to do it right.

July 9

"I am patient with myself and rest when I need to."

Balance is important to remember. Eating right, resting, de-stressing and relaxing must be balanced with working hard. Be sure to take time to recharge, there are many benefits including increasing your creativity and even improving your immune system.

July 10

"I am feeling exceptionally strong today."

If you are not feeling strong today, try a couple of jumping jacks to invigorate you. Try going to bed early and waking up early to help give you more energy.

July 11

"I am proud of myself for all I have accomplished so far."

Applaud yourself! The beginning is the hardest part, you are already headed in the right direction towards your goals.

July 12

"I am resilient and nothing can stop me."

Resilience is the ability to spring back into shape quickly after a setback, or not bending at all. Whatever comes along, quickly learn from it and move on. Never stop pursuing your goals.

July 13

"I always have enough money."

This affirmation will give you comfort in knowing that whatever you need, you can find a way to afford it. Once money starts to roll in, it doesn't stop.

July 14

"I am on my journey to success."

The journey may be long and have twists and turns along the way. It can be hard to know where you are on your journey but have faith you will arrive at your destination.

July 15

"All is well."

If you are a worrier like me, or an over-thinker, this affirmation will put you at ease and quiet your mind.

July 16

"I am focused on my goals."

Removing distractions from your life is an essential part of focusing on your goals. You need to put your energy into achieving your dreams. Try to eliminate time-wasting bad habits, cut out unimportant TV shows and use your energy towards working on your plan.

July 17

"My bravery gets me where I want to go."

Bravery is using your courage and mental strength to face fear or difficulty. Be strong, and persevere through unfavorable circumstances.

July 18

"My success depends on my efforts."

Consistent and persistent effort and action will move you along your path. If you are feeling like success is still elusive, maybe it's time to put in more effort. Rest when you need to and work harder when you can.

July 19

"I celebrate my independence and my ability to follow my dreams."

There are few greater feelings than being independent and able to do what you choose without having to run it by anymore. Be proud of yourself for having the courage to follow your dreams.

July 20

"Failure is my ally."

Any sports hall of famer will tell you that the only reason they did well so many times is because they also failed more times than anyone else. They just tried more times than their peers. Do more. Do not fear failure, in fact, welcome it and learn from it. Failure is just important as success because we can learn from it and come back stronger and smarter.

July 21

"My actions today, guarantee my results in the future."

The way to a successful future is to stop talking and take action now! What can you do today that will help your plan to your goals?

July 22

"My success is infinite."

You really can have all the success. But only if you eliminate doubt. Doubt is the killer of success, make a decision to arm yourself with affirmations close at hand when doubt creeps in.

July 23

"I will show up today and every day."

95% of success is just showing up. Being there and being ready to get to work or to be of service will guarantee success.

July 24

"I am systematically doing positive actions according to my plan to reach my goals."

Make a to-do list of things that you need to do next. Keep it on your wall until each thing is accomplished and you can cross them all off. If you have been working on your plan for a while, it's a great time to do a check-in and make a list of actions that you need to do now.

July 25

"I trust myself."

Removing any lingering self-doubt is an important step in trusting yourself. Some things you can do to increase trust in yourself are: write down the things that you like about yourself, trust your intuition and follow your desires.

July 26

"I only put healthy food in my body."

Fruits and vegetables are healthy, sugar and fat are not. It's pretty simple. Save the indulgences for a special occasion, try to make healthy choices on regular days.

July 27

"I am transforming my life."

Every day your life is changing. You are working towards your goals and becoming a new person. Affirmations, vision boards and a supportive network of people will help you achieve your transformation.

July 28

"I am strong and brave."

If you ever feel doubt creeping in, this affirmation will stop it in its tracks. I say this if I wake up in the early morning worrying about everything that needs to be done.

July 29

"I easily find all the resources that I need."

Trust that what you need will come to you at the right time. As soon as you start looking, you will find what you need.

July 30

"I believe there is enough money for everyone."

More money for you doesn't mean you are taking anything away from anyone else. Life is an all-you-can-eat buffet, take what you need and others are free to do the same.

July 31

"New doors are opening for me."

You may have to knock on a few doors before some open for you. Create your opportunities by looking for them. If you are not finding any new doors, you might have to close some old doors before new ones start to open for you.

8

AUGUST

August 1

"I generously give money to those in need."

The old practice of tithing, or giving a percentage of your income to those in need, may not be practical today. I encourage you to find a cause, Covenant house for teens, an animal rescue, or St. Jude's hospital for sick kids. Something powerful happens when you share with those in need. You will be put in charge of more money to distribute at your discretion.

August 2

"I am enthusiastic about my life."

Enthusiasm is contagious. When you exude enthusiasm is spreads to those around you and magic can happen. Choose your team of helpful people carefully and help to energize them with your positive, enthusiastic attitude.

August 3

"I do what makes my heart happy."

When your heart is happy, you are the sun in your own solar system, people are drawn to you because of your authentic joy. Not only is a happy heart essential for your bliss, but doctors attribute some element of health to having a happy heart.

August 4

"I choose to focus on myself and my goals."

Free yourself from distractions, instead of engaging in meaningless time fillers, make some choices to do things that help your plan. Try some behind-the-scenes research or meeting up with like-minded colleagues.

August 5

"I believe my talents and skills will earn me the money I desire."

The way to sustainable riches is by trading a product or service for money. What can you offer people? Spend some time thinking about a skill you have, that you enjoy, that you can offer to others.

August 6

"I love and appreciate my body."

Exercising and eating right will help you fight off illness and stress. Take care of your most important asset. You will want to be healthy to enjoy the fruits of your labor in the years to come.

August 7

"I am creating financial freedom for myself."

I think everyone in the world desires to be financially free. The difference is you have a burning desire and a solid plan to get there. You are also fortunate to have opportunities available to you to make this a reality. Do some extra work on your plan today.

August 8

"I am persistent and will not stop until I reach my goals."

Persistence pays off. Persistence is the vehicle to take you on your path to your goals. You can rest but don't you quit.

August 9

"Practicing gratitude brings me joy."

The benefits of practicing gratitude are nearly endless. They include, happier emotions including joy, health benefits, a gateway to abundance, making others around you happier and an increase in our self-esteem.

August 10

"I will get it done."

If you are like me, I sometimes start to worry about a project that I've been putting off or that is coming up. I repeat this affirmation to help me finish it quickly. Cross it off your to-do list!

August 11

"I am living my own truth and I believe my dreams are important."

Others will have different dreams and likely don't share yours. Do what makes you happy. Try to distance yourself from unsupportive people and find a new team of like-minded people that are helpful and supportive on your journey to your goals.

August 12

"I do not accept anyone's negative behavior, it flows past me and leaves."

When change starts to happen in your life, don't be surprised if jealousy surges up from so-called friends or even family members. See it for what it is, let it go through you and continue working on your plan to reach your goals.

August 13

"Luck is on my side."

Luck is considered to be favorable conditions that are brought merely by chance rather than by one's own efforts. It has been shown however, that one can create their own luck. The best way is by hard work, also by being positive and being on the lookout for luck.

August 14

"Today, I am the best version of myself."

We live many versions of ourselves over the years. It's time for the best You 5.0. Some ways to accomplish this is: by listing your favorite affirmations and reading them regularly, by eliminating anything unhealthy or toxic, and by appreciating failure and learning from it.

August 15

"I have a burning desire to achieve my goals."

Burning desire is what will guarantee your unwavering commitment to reaching your goals. You must make your desire so strong that quitting or failing is not an option. Envision how you will feel with your new house or pool, look at your vision board as much as possible.

August 16

"My skills are exceptional and I am financially rewarded for them."

Try to focus on quality, go the extra mile with your products or services. Your customers and clients will appreciate it and they are the bread and butter on your journey to riches.

August 17

"I am always attracting abundance."

Gratitude is the best way to attract abundance. Be grateful for all you have and continue looking at your vision board regularly to attract an even more abundant future. Giving your extra money away to people that need it is also a sure-fire way to increase the abundance headed your way.

August 18

"Amazing things are entering my life."

Small miracles are happening every day, you just need to look for them. Miracles of life, love and nature are all around us. Appreciating the small amazements will bring bigger ones into your life.

August 19

"I invest in myself and in my future."

Find ways of planting more seeds today that you can reap in the future. Whether it is investing a small amount financially, buying some starter supplies for your business or taking a course in something you are interested in. Do it now, your future self will thank you!

August 20

"Success is magnetically attracted to me."

What is success? Success is the state of meeting your desired goals. It is the opposite of failure. The secret to success is planning, hard work and learning from failure. When failure comes up, embrace it and learn from it, we are ready for success now!

August 21

"My goals are BIG, and I can't wait to accomplish them."

Why make your goals BIG? Big goals get us excited, they force us to make a really good plan and they force us to do more and do it faster. Once you reach a goal, you will be thankful that you made it big.

August 22

"Today, I will practice gratitude for the achievements I have already made."

Gratitude will give your joy. Thank yourself and others that have helped you for what you have already done. Being gracious will allow additional, bigger achievements to become your reality.

August 23

"I attract people into my life that help me reach my goals."

You will need a helpful team of positive people to reach your goals. For every big accomplishment I've done in my life, I can count at least 10+ characters that have been essential in getting it done. The lawyer that does your paper-work, the supplier you found online or the helper you hire. Choose your team wisely and treat them kindly.

August 24

"I receive unexpected money."

Check your bank account or go for a walk and look around. Consider buying someone a cup of coffee or helping someone else with extra money you find. I lost 50 dollars once, I hope the person that found it did something positive with it.

August 25

"I eat well and exercise regularly."

A healthy lifestyle will help your sleep and your mood. You need to be on top of your game for your journey to your goals. It might be long and you never know what challenges you will have to overcome, so be ready!

August 26

"I accept myself unconditionally."

In order to accept yourself unconditionally, you must know yourself through and through, even the darkest corners. Spending time alone will uncover your deepest feelings, once you have done this, then accept and never judge yourself. Be your own supporter and love all parts of yourself.

August 27

"Prosperity flows towards me."

Prosperity is very dynamic in nature, it comes from an exchange of your goods or services for what you want in return, usually money. In order to flourish and thrive you need to keep the dynamic going, give away your extra to keep prosperity flowing back to you.

August 28

"I comfort myself and give myself everything I need."

You are really stretching yourself on your journey to your goals. You are learning a lot and changing a lot in a short amount of time. Give yourself what you need to feel comforted and be patient with yourself as you travel to your dreams.

August 29

"I am in control of my life and my decisions."

You may need to become aware of healthy boundaries with others. Educate yourself if needed, so that you know where your healthy boundaries are. If you are finding that others are not respecting your life and decisions, then you are free to demand respect. It is your life, no one else's.

August 30

"I am becoming mentally stronger every day."

Don't be defeated by fear, if you feel it creeping in, find your favorite affirmations and repeat them as often as possible. As you stumble towards success, you will become stronger every day, remain positive and continue to challenge yourself to try and be open to new ideas. Slowly but surely, you will become mentally resilient.

August 31

"My confidence in myself continues to grow every day."

Self-confidence is a bonus you will get from your journey. As you continue to make good decisions and work hard, you will accept and trust yourself more each day.

9

SEPTEMBER

September 1

"Today, I attract miracles into my life."

Miracles can happen, look around, they are happening every day. Flowers blooming in the spring, children being born, people healing illness. A positive, clean mind is a garden for miracles.

September 2

"I take time every day to improve my health."

Your body is your biggest asset, you need it to last a long time. Make time every day to eat healthily and exercise. Put a reminder or even two in your phone so that you can stop what you are doing and focus on your health, even for a short time each day.

September 3

"Having lots of money is normal for me."

By repeating this affirmation, your brain will think that it is normal for you to have lots of money and your reality will be forced to catch up.

September 4

"I believe in myself and my skills and talents."

You have to be the first one to believe in yourself before anyone else will. By believing in yourself, you build your self-confidence. Your skills and talents are unique, you just need to figure out how you can share them with others.

September 5

"I am creating prosperity in my life by taking action."

There is no time like the present to take action. Have a look at your action plan for your path to your goals, what can you do today to work on your plan?

September 6

"Success comes quickly and easily to me."

Stop trying so hard at things that aren't meant to be. Many success stories happen after someone has given up completely on forcing things that just suck their energy. Once you give up unrealistic plans, something happens, it clears the way for true success, built on things you enjoy and love to do.

September 7

"I always give my best effort and it is enough."

Give all you have when you are making a product or providing a service. Go above and beyond, customers will greatly appreciate this as most quality has slumped in recent years. Loyal customers are a big part of your team.

September 8

"I see abundance everywhere I look."

Some suggestions for seeing and feeling extra abundance are: start a savings account or even a "spare" coin or bill collection in a container, give back to others if you have extra money and try to enjoy the fine things you own. Use your nice dishes for no reason or put on your fancy clothes to go grocery shopping.

September 9

"I give my body the nourishment it needs to heal and maintain health."

Your body wants to be healthy. It is its natural state. Giving it proper nutrients, cutting out sugar and fat and exercising regularly will give your body what it needs to heal and maintain itself.

September 10

"I believe in myself."

Believing in yourself can make or break your plans. Anything you can imagine, is something you can achieve. Believe you have the ability to do it. If you don't, who will? You must be your biggest supporter.

September 11

"New ideas and opportunities arrive just when I need them."

New opportunities don't come along every day, when they do, be sure to seize them. As you travel on your path to your goals keep your eyes open so you can recognize a great opportunity when one presents itself.

September 12

"I believe everything is unfolding as it is meant to be."

Having faith in a universal power will give you reassurance that everything is working perfectly. If things aren't moving as fast as you would like, be patient. Take whatever small steps you can take today to move you closer to your goals.

September 13

"I receive new sources of income."

Maybe an opportunity will come to you or maybe you need to create your own opportunity. There are many ways of generating new income streams: start a YouTube Channel, create a website that sells something or go door to door with a homemade craft or creation.

September 14

"I am following my heart."

Don't be afraid to follow your heart. Fear is the biggest road-block, fear of what people will think or fear of what problems may lay ahead. Be brave, your heart will always lead you in the right direction if you are courageous enough to listen.

September 15

"I am full of energy today."

If you need an energy boost today, try taking a walk or drinking a healthy juice drink. Other things that suck up our energy are clutter and not having boundaries with pushy people.

September 16

"I am confident in my abilities."

Accepting yourself and realizing what you are capable of and what you are not, will help you really maximize your abilities. Once you know what you are good at, go for it! Make the most of what you are good at and what you enjoy.

September 17

"I balance my work, play and rest."

Balance is more important than ever these days. Family, work, and other commitments are relentless and demanding. Be your own scheduler, you may have to write down a schedule and stick to it. Make sure you can fit in everything that is important to you, including time for health and rest.

September 18

"I remain optimistic regardless of any challenges that arise."

Optimism is having faith in your successful outcome. When challenges arise, try to focus on the solution rather than the problem, don't dwell on it, fix it and move on.

September 19

"I am free of excuses."

Excuses are a barricade to success. Excuses will keep you stuck, they are like a flat tire on the road to your dreams and goals. They are useless, throw them in the garbage and get on with your plan.

September 20

"My potential is limitless."

There is no end to what you can achieve. You already have some goals you are working on, but after you accomplish those, you can set new, even bigger ones.

September 21

"I can solve any problem because I am smart."

Take responsibility for problems that arise, this means "responding-ably". You have the power to fix things, you know yourself well and can come up with a solution.

September 22

"The seeds I sow today, I will reap soon."

Sometimes it's hard to imagine the fruits of our labor. Continue to tend and care for the small seeds of success you are planting. Trust that the actions you are taking today, will pay off in the future, be patient.

September 23

"I am excited about the journey to my goals and welcome everything along my path."

Hopefully, your plan consists of something you are enthusiastic about. It makes all the difference when challenges arise.

September 24

"Good things are happening to me."

Focusing on the good things throughout the day will only bring more good. What we focus on expands and becomes more powerful. Take note and give gratitude for the small blessings that come up through the day.

September 25

"I have abundant vitality because I am aligned with my purpose."

Do what you love and you will always love what you do. Once you find your true passion, whether it is your full-time job, a side gig or a hobby, you will be invigorated with a new energy. One that comes from deep inside and gives you joy.

September 26

"I am persistent and will never give up on my goals."

Quitting is not an option. If you are ever feeling unmotivated, it's time to step up your plans to reach your goals. I suggest making a new additional vision board with some fabulous photos of houses, cars, relationship photos or whatever it is that you desire. Let's get that drive back so we can get what we want!

September 27

"I am proud of my bravery."

Your behavior and your character are what define you as brave. Since you are making courageous steps to reach your goals, you should feel content with and grateful to yourself for getting you where you want to go, to your dreams!

September 28

"Being wealthy is normal for me."

This affirmation will make your mind think wealth is normal and already here. You will feel like you have already reached your financial goals. Once your mindset is programmed to that of a wealthy person, your reality and your bank account will quickly catch up.

September 29

"I trust my intuition."

Trust your gut, if someone or something feels off, then scrap it. It is a great feeling to walk away, or toward, what we determine is the best for ourselves. As you continue to make good decisions towards reaching your goals, your intuition will get sharper, and easier to uncover and understand. Try to listen to that quiet voice telling you what is best for yourself.

September 30

"I am enjoying NOW."

The present is called the present because it is a gift. Although we have big plans for the future, now is all we are guaranteed. Enjoy the moment, it is powerful. If you need to change something or do something important, don't wait. Do it now.

10

OCTOBER

October 1

"I am taking care of my body."

Rest, exercise and diet are so important to your body. You only get one body, it will be with you your whole life. Sometimes we take better care of our car than our body. Time to realize what is important and make time, and a list, to keep us on track to form some healthy habits for our body's well-being.

October 2

"My actions are courageous."

It takes courage and bravery to ditch the status quo and go in search of a way to reach our goals. Continue to take action, this is the only way to achieve success and reach your dreams.

October 3

"I make great choices."

I used to struggle between choice A and choice B. As I got older, it became easier. Why? I learned to trust my intuition, to listen to that tiny voice inside, and also to believe that even if my choice doesn't work out how I wished, I will learn from it and come back stronger.

October 4

"I am being helped."

When we bravely start on our path to our goals, something happens. It's as if the forces of the universe recognize your desire and help you along your way. Start and you will be helped.

October 5

"I attract the wealth I desire."

Some tips to help you become a money magnet are: count your money regularly, visualize yourself being wealthy and keep track of all the prosperity that comes to you and give much gratitude when it does.

October 6

"I feel strong and full of energy."

Some ways to help you feel strong and energetic are: take a walk, declutter, follow a powerful influencer on social media, clean up your house or listen to some invigorating music.

October 7

"I am safe."

Sometimes anxiety and worries about the future get the better of us. Time to comfort and calm yourself with this affirmation. How will you pay a certain bill? Not to worry, you will be safe no matter what and you will figure out a way to meet your obligations.

October 8

"I am attracting love into my life."

Be the embodiment of love. Spread it wherever you go. Love is a two-way street, in order to receive it, you must give it. If you are looking for your soulmate, spend time envisioning them and how you will feel when you meet them.

October 9

"I conquer anxious feelings with action."

Action is the killer of anxiety. If you are feeling anxious, it is because something needs to be done and you are putting it off or not confronting it head-on. Be brave. Deal with it so you can move on.

October 10

"I am open to limitless possibilities."

Once abundance starts to flow in your life, you never know what could happen. When you are aligned with your purpose and are doing things that are best for you, great things will just continue to grow and expand.

October 11

"I am creating powerful change."

When you make the decision to create change in your life, there is no turning back. It's a one-way ticket to success. Your old life is not coming back, be excited for the new things coming to you slowly but surely.

October 12

"I fulfill my own needs and wants."

You will need a team of supportive people along your journey, but don't count on any of them to fulfill your needs or your wants. That is up to you. If you want a coffee or need a day off, arrange it for yourself, no need to explain anything to anyone.

October 13

"I attract helpful people into my life."

Some people genuinely want to see you succeed and some do not. When you find a selfless person that wants to help you succeed, they are like gold, treat them as such and be eternally grateful for their unconditional help and support.

October 14

"Every day that I am alive is a gift."

Although we have big plans for the future, the power of NOW is incredible. Enjoy today, call someone you love, you never know when it will be your last chance.

October 15

"I am the architect of my future."

Now that you are in charge of creating your future, and reaching your goals, get ready for change. Getting used to change is a funny thing because change is always changing. Get comfortable with change and embrace it. Your journey, is a journey, along the way everything changes.

October 16

"Brilliant ideas come easily to me."

Some people believe that brilliant ideas come to us by chance. Regardless of how we get them, we need to act on them in such a way as to make them useful to other people. If we can't make use of the brilliant idea, then it will either fade away or someone else will get the idea and use it.

October 17

"My dreams are becoming my reality."

Every day that you are working towards your goals, is one day closer to your dreams. Continue to work hard, don't make excuses and learn from challenges.

October 18

"I have faith in myself."

As you get to know your strengths, you can focus on what you are good at and make it part of your plans. If you have a talent, put it to work and earn some money towards your goals. Believe in your own abilities to be successful.

October 19

"My success is beginning now."

The intentional actions that you choose today will determine your results. Choose some actions that will get you results that help you reach your goals. Do them now.

October 20

"I attract positive and supportive people into my life."

Practice being the positive person you want to attract. Clear out any negativity, be honest with yourself and others and practice being supportive, this will attract supportive and positive people.

October 21

"Incredible opportunities are always coming to me."

When opportunity comes calling, be ready to greet it. Be on guard for great opportunities and when they present themselves, go for it! If you fail to recognize an opportunity someone else will seize it from you.

October 22

"I am patient and understanding with myself and others."

Being in control of our own emotions will help with patience when challenges arise. Sometimes deadlines are missed or things just don't go as planned. Endure the difficulty until a solution can be found, in short, make the best of it and learn what you can.

October 23

"I am motivated and focused."

If you are having a hard time staying motivated, break down your goal into some smaller steps and reward yourself regularly for the effort you put in.

October 24

"I am grateful for the money I receive."

Money loves attention. When you receive money, count it, look at it or enjoy the numbers in your banking app. This will help keep the flow of money coming towards you.

October 25

"I listen to my body and hear what it needs to be healthy."

Is there something you've been ignoring? Maybe you're overtired or have put on a few extra pounds from lack of exercise. Make a bigger effort to be healthy, make a list of daily goals and stick to it.

October 26

"I am financially free."

Imagine what it will feel like to not have any bills, mortgage or rent to pay. To be able to buy anything or travel anywhere you want. To have security for the rest of your life. The more you think about it, the closer it will come to your reality.

October 27

"Today, I feel joyful and I spread it to others."

Being thankful for the small things around you will help you feel joy today. Try thanking others for being good friends, it will help spread the feeling of joy.

October 28

"I make healthy choices to nourish my body."

If you have a few guilty pleasures, try replacing them with a healthier choice. There really are great products that are also healthy. Be open to trying something new.

October 29

"I choose to be happy."

Make the choice to focus on happiness, not on things that annoy you. Instead of cursing in traffic, try to think understanding, kind thoughts instead. Count your blessings and try to smile today.

October 30

"I am excited for the opportunities today brings."

You have many choices today: which way to walk to work, who you talk to, what you read or watch for entertainment.

With each choice, different opportunities will present themselves, enjoy the adventure of today.

October 31

"I am productive and positive."

Start being productive by solving your existing problems and stop wasting time. By solving problems, the door opens to positivity and leads the way to being really productive.

11

NOVEMBER

November 1

"I have all the energy I need to accomplish my goals."

It may seem like the path to your goals is a long one. Think of driving a car on a journey, you must focus on what is in front of you now so that you reach your destination safely. Some tips for more energy are: drink more water, only drink coffee in the morning and exercise.

November 2

"I control my thoughts."

Control your thoughts or they will control you. Affirmations will help you control your thoughts and program your mind so you can get the results you desire.

November 3

"My life is an adventure and I plan the course."

Try to enjoy all the ups and downs that come with being alive. You can chart the course by setting some big goals, but the events on your path are yet to be determined.

November 4

"I radiate success."

Fake it until you make it. Imagine you have already succeeded, how will you feel? What will you wear? Will you spend time worrying about little unimportant things, or get on with bigger things that further contribute to your success?

November 5

"Change is easy and gets me closer to my goals."

Change is not always easy but to reach your goals there will be constant change. So if you can make yourself believe that change is easy and enjoy change, you will have an easier time achieving your dreams.

November 6

"I am attracting supportive people into my life."

Try to be the person you want to attract. Try being supportive to those around you, not judging and only offering positive comments.

November 7

"Money flows to me from all directions."

Multiple streams of income are a great idea if one of your goals is to have more money. Try selling something that you have made: wood-working or plants from your garden are some ideas.

November 8

"I create new healthy habits to replace old outdated ones."

Your journey is dynamic, you might be surprised when you realize some of your old habits are not needed anymore. Watching TV before bed can be replaced with watching an educational video or reading something that will help you achieve your goals faster.

November 9

"I am grateful for all my experiences and achievements."

Gratitude will bring you more positive opportunities. Praise yourself for what you have accomplished so far. All the events that have happened in your life have made you the person you are today. Be grateful for all of them.

November 10

"The extra money I receive helps others."

Be sure to give away some of your money to help others. When you do this, it triggers something. The universe will give you more money to divide up how you see fit. Try to find a cause or a charity that is important to you.

November 11

"I believe in myself."

Know that you can overcome anything. You must support yourself 100% in order to get yourself to your goals. They are your goals and you are the only one that can get yourself there.

November 12

"I will persevere until I reach my goals."

It is the struggle and the hard times that will really make you appreciate success once you arrive. Keep on, keeping on, it will be worth it one day.

November 13

"I am confident in myself and believe in my abilities."

Every challenge along the way will make you stronger and increase your self-confidence. Don't focus on mistakes of the past, learn from them and use them to propel yourself forwards.

November 14

"I am unstoppable."

Think of yourself as a bulldozer, slow, strong and unstoppable. Slowly pushing everything unneeded aside and making a nice path towards your dreams.

November 15

"I am open to new solutions."

Is there a challenge that keeps reoccurring? It's time for some good old-fashioned brainstorming. Take a pen and paper and write the challenge in the middle with a circle around it, draw branches coming off it with more circles with some possible solutions inside them. You never know what you will come up with.

November 16

"Magic is all around me."

If you can't feel everyday magic today, try gardening in the dirt, doing some hands-on finger painting or watching the sun rise or set. Magic is found in childish, simple pleasures.

November 17

"I read my goals every day so that they become who I am now."

The more you look at your vision board, read and write out your goals and practice your daily affirmations, the more you are reprogramming your mind. You are actually becoming these things that once were only a dream.

November 18

"I am happy with myself, and I am the only one that matters."

What others think of you is not your concern. A LOT of energy is wasted on people caring about what others think.

November 19

"I am creating incredible wealth."

Spend some more time investigating the three main types of income. They are earned, portfolio and passive income. Which one do you need to expand?

November 20

"I feel fit and strong."

You will need energy to complete your journey to your goals. Drink more water, exercise daily and make healthy dietary choices. Write down a daily list of goals if you need to.

November 21

"My bravery gets me through anything."

Be confident that you will stand tall and fight when you need to. Your courage will get through whatever comes your way.

November 22

"I am attracting new opportunities into my life."

Look in the areas of your passions for new opportunities. Try volunteering or learning more about one of your favorite topics to create some new opportunities of your own.

November 23

"I will keep trying and never give up until I reach my goals."

If at first you don't succeed, try again! You will come back stronger and wiser. Use failure as a stepping stone to success, if you are feeling defeated, take a rest to regroup and then get back at it!

November 24

"I am aligned with my purpose."

When you are aware of your passions and what you are truly excited about and meant to do in your life, things will fall into place. Not only will you thoroughly enjoy your days but there are also numerous ways to make your passion into a way to earn income.

November 25

"I create my circumstances with the intentional actions I take."

Focus on your ideas and thoughts of your goals, and remember the plan you have to get there. Take action today that will help move you along your path.

November 26

"I trade my hard work for an abundance of money."

True wealth can only come from selling a product or providing a service. Every second of your day is valuable, find a way to get monetarily rewarded for trading your valuable time.

November 27

"Everything is working out perfectly for me."

We can't always see the big picture, nor do we know how all the pieces will fit together. Trust that now that you are aligned with your dreams and goals, everything is working itself out to benefit you.

November 28

"I release all that doesn't serve me, to make room for what I desire now."

Sometimes we have to make room for what is coming. If you feel unproductive or blocked, it's time for some housecleaning. Either mentally release what isn't working for you anymore or physically give some old furniture to the goodwill and make room for what you want now.

November 29

"I am my biggest supporter."

Be the parent to yourself that you always wished you had. Tell yourself: "you can do it" and "I believe in you'.

November 30

"Attaining my goals is so close I can feel them."

Once you start working on your plan to your goals, you are effectively becoming part of your success. You may not be there yet, but you are getting close!

12

DECEMBER

December 1

"I am achieving whatever I set my mind to."

Remember, your brain is the original computer, if you give it the right input, the output is almost certainly guaranteed. Be careful what you put into your brain today, it will take your directions and act on them.

December 2

"My dreams are becoming my reality."

When you reach your goals, what will you do differently? Go to a fancy restaurant or buy some nice clothes? Treat yourself now, it will make reaching your dreams that much easier and natural.

December 3

"I am productive."

Some people find multi-tasking productive, while others get overwhelmed by it. Do what works for you, you may need to make a daily to-do list and just do one thing at a time and then enjoy crossing it off.

December 4

"My confidence gets me through tough days."

Be confident in yourself and believe that you will be there to pick yourself up and dust yourself off when needed. There will always be tough days, try to take care of yourself so you can recover quickly and get back at it.

December 5

"I enjoy meeting other people and make new friends easily."

Even though you are responsible for achieving your goals, there will be many characters that help you along the way. Be open to networking and meeting new supportive people with a similar mindset.

December 6

"I am comfortable in my own skin."

Stop caring about what others think. You know yourself the best and you know what you are capable of. Working on personal issues and weaknesses privately will help you feel more confident with yourself.

December 7

"I am my own hero."

Stop waiting for the perfect person to enter your life, fix everything and rescue you. You are your own hero, be the person that fixes everything and rescue yourself.

December 8

"I motivate myself."

Are you self-motivated? If your answer is no, is time to dig deep and find a passion project. Think back to the best times in your life, what were you doing? When you are engaging in a meaningful project or venture, motivation will be inherent.

December 9

"My actions take me closer to my greater purpose."

You can only do so much in a day, choose wisely and focus on actions that will get you where you want to go.

December 10

"I am financially free."

Try to save a bit of your income and pay off your debts. Give away some of your hard-earned money and always look for opportunities to create more income.

December 11

"I am proud of myself and what I have already accomplished."

Be proud of how far you have come and how hard you are trying. Be proud of your goal setting and efforts thus far. It takes a lot of courage to follow your dreams.

December 12

"I take care of myself and rest when I need to."

Listen to your body, when it's time to rest be sure that you do. Your body will thank you and be rejuvenated.

December 13

"I can barely contain my excitement for the future."

Take another look at your vision board, imagine how you will feel when you achieve your goals. How will you feel driving your new car or moving into your new house?

December 14

"I am ambitious."

Ambition means always striving to reach your goals. Never stopping. Hard work, perseverance and dedication will get you there.

December 15

"I am ready to receive abundance in all areas of my life."

Giving gratitude for the small things and clearing the way to welcome new opportunities in all areas, will invite abundance into your life.

December 16

"Every challenge that happens gets me one step closer to my goals."

Think of the path to your goals as riddled with challenges. If we can learn from the challenge we can move past it and continue on. If we bypass the lesson and try to take a short-cut, unlearned challenges will always show up again.

December 17

"Today I will give my body what it needs."

Do you need more sleep? Take a nap today. Do you need some exercise? Go for a walk. Do you need to just sit and do nothing? Whatever comes to your mind, do that.

December 18

"My new energy is strong!"

At times when I've had a big energy shift in my own life, many things and people around me have acted strangely. My computer broke down because I was inspired and used it so much, my tooth chipped because I was exuberant with energy. People in your life may not respond positively, be kind and carry on.

December 19

"Money comes to me easily."

Make yourself a money magnet. Remember sustainable wealth can only come from providing a valuable product or service to others. Practice gratitude for the money you receive in exchange for your product or service. Visualize money coming to you easily.

December 20

"I appreciate everything I have in my life."

Focus on the good in your life and appreciate it. Don't dwell on the negatives that pop up. Just fix them, appreciate what you have learned and move on. Appreciating everything will open the door to what you desire.

December 21

"My inner light is growing brighter."

It is always darkest before the dawn. It is the darker times that make us appreciate when light returns. Enjoy the Winter Solstice, for tomorrow longer days, will return.

December 22

"I feel calm, confident, and powerful."

There is no need to worry, everything is working as it should be, be patient, your goals are getting closer and closer to you every day. Enjoy where you are and be proud of your accomplishments.

December 23

"Everything in my life is a blessing."

Things that you might think are just a nuisance, are actually blessings. You can learn just as much from bothersome things, as from favorable events.

December 24

"I am able to concentrate on my work so I can reach my goals."

Eliminating distractions will help with concentrating your energy. Some other tips for improving concentration are: take an exercise break, play some brain concentration games or turn off music or noise while you are working.

December 25

"I practice giving and receiving."

Giving and receiving are two sides of the same coin. It is important to practice both separately so that they can flow together and keep you in tune with universal abundance.

December 26

"I inspire others."

Be the inspiring person you wish you knew. Don't micromanage others, help them to find purpose in what they do as well. By helping and inspiring others we can transform our lives as well as the lives of others.

December 27

"I continue to follow my plan and get closer to my goals every day."

We don't know exactly how long our journey is to reach our desired goals. As long as you stay on your path and follow your plan, you will get there, one step at a time.

December 28

"Miracles are happening in my life."

Clearing out space in your mind and your life will open the door to miracles. If you want to see a miracle, watch the sun rising and setting or plant some seeds and watch what happens.

December 29

"I am achieving my financial goals, and I will not stop until I do."

Persistence and confidence will get you there. Know that you have all that is needed to reach your goals. Try putting up some more pictures of money around your house.

December 30

"I easily attract all that I desire."

Focus on your vision board, make it bigger if you need to. Continue to make time for focussing on your desires and keep manifesting them until they arrive.

December 31

"Everything I start, I finish strong."

When things get tough, will you settle for where you are, or will you push through and finish strong? The last few seconds of a race determine the winner and quite often the most points in sports games are scored in the final minutes. Keep going, the finish line is near!

Congratulations! You have finished an incredible year. Hopefully, you are feeling empowered and closer to your goals. I would now encourage you to update your goals. Maybe you have achieved some small goals and your bigger goals are still in progress. Make a New Year's commitment to start another updated vision board and read this book again with your current goals in mind. All the best for the New Year!

Made in the USA
Monee, IL
12 January 2023

25091540R00088